Space

Planets

Charlotte Guillain

HEINEMANN LIBRARY

www.heinemannlibrary.co.uk

Visit our website to find out more information about Heinemann Library books.

To order:
☎ Phone 44 (0) 1865 888066
▤ Send a fax to 44 (0) 1865 314091
▥ Visit the Heinemann Bookshop at www.heinemannlibrary.co.uk to browse our catalogue and order online.

Heinemann Library is an imprint of Capstone Global Library Limited, a company incorporated in England and Wales having its registered office at 7 Pilgrim Street, London, EC4V 6LB – Registered company number: 6695582

Heinemann is a registered trademark of Pearson Education Limited, under licence to Capstone Global Library Limited

Edited by Siân Smith, Rebecca Rissman, and Charlotte Guillain
Designed by Joanna Hinton-Malivoire
Picture research by Tracy Cummins and Heather Mauldin
Production by Duncan Gilbert
Originated by Heinemann Library
Printed and bound in China by South China Printing Company Ltd

ISBN 978 0 431 02045 7
13 12 11 10 09
10 9 8 7 6 5 4 3 2 1

British Library Cataloguing in Publication Data

Guillain, Charlotte
Planets. - (Space)
1. Planets - Juvenile literature
I. Title
523.4

Acknowledgements

We would would like to thank the following for permission to reproduce photographs: ©Age Fotostock p.7; Getty Images pp. 8 (©MPI/Stringer), 15, 17, 19, 23c (©Stocktrek Images); Jupiter Images p.6 (©Chris Walsh); NASA p.10 (©JPL); Photo Researchers Inc pp.4 (©SPL), 11 (©Science Source/NASA), 14, 16 (©Detlev van Ravensswaay), 18 (©SPL), 23a (©Detlev van Ravensswaay); Photolibrary p.9 (©Ron Chapple Stock); Shutterstock pp.5 (©Zastol'skiy Victor Leonidovich), 12 (©Patrick Hermans), 13 (©Sebastian Kaulitzki), 21 (©Oorka), 22 (©Andrea Danti), 23b (©Sebastian Kaulitzki).

Front cover photograph reproduced with permission of NASA (©JPL/USGS). Back cover photograph reproduced with permission of Shutterstock (©Patrick Hermans).

Every effort has been made to contact copyright holders of material reproduced in this book. Any omissions will be rectified in subsequent printings if notice is given to the publishers.

Contents

Planets

Planets are in space.

Space is up above the sky.

What are planets like?

Planets are giant objects in space.

6

Planets are shaped like balls.

Some planets are made of rock.
Mercury, Venus, Earth, and Mars are
made of rock.

Some planets are made of gas.

Jupiter, Saturn, Uranus, and Neptune are made of gas.

moons

Some planets have moons. Jupiter has many moons.

rings

Some planets have rings. Saturn has rings.

The Solar System

There are eight planets in the
Solar System.

the Sun

The planets move around, or orbit, the Sun.

Some planets are close to the Sun.

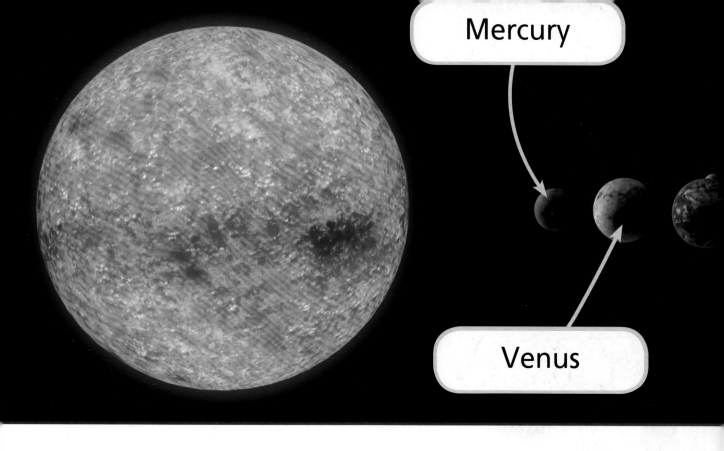

Mercury

Venus

Mercury and Venus are planets close
to the Sun.

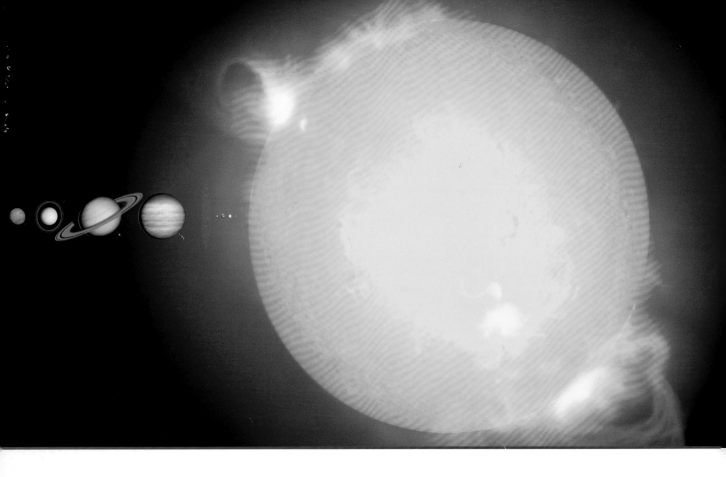

Some planets are far from the Sun.

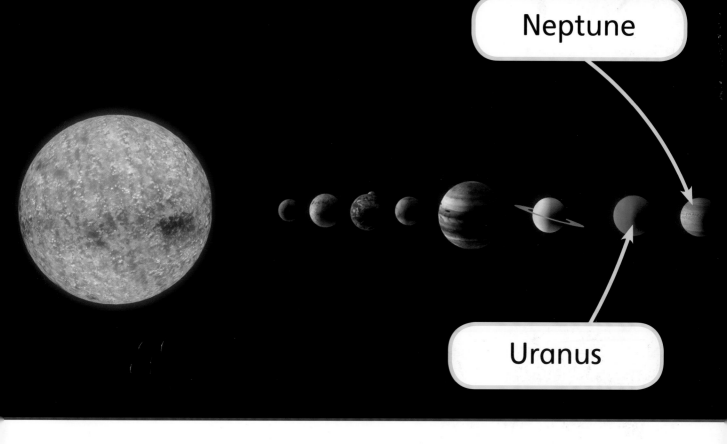

Neptune

Uranus

Uranus and Neptune are planets far from the Sun.

Earth

Earth

Earth is a planet.

We live on planet Earth.

Earth is in space.

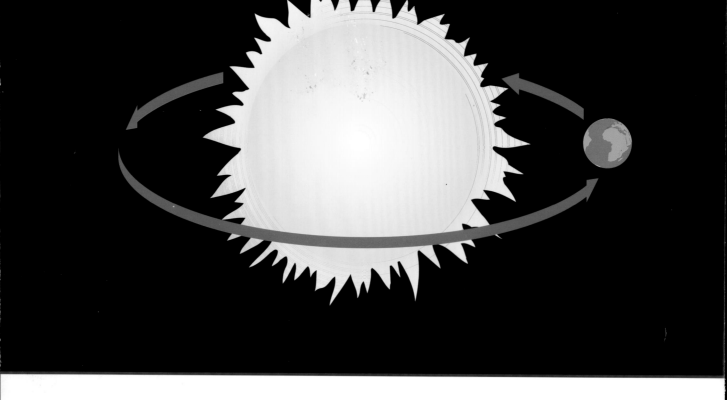

Earth orbits the Sun.

Earth has a moon.

Can you remember?

How many planets are there in the Solar System?

22

Answer on p.24

Picture glossary

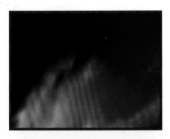

gas not solid like wood or liquid like water. Air is a gas that we breathe in but cannot see.

orbit move around

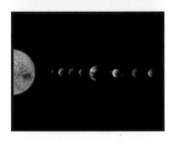

Solar System the name for the Sun and the eight planets that move around it

Index

Answer to question on p.22: There are eight planets in the Solar System.

Notes to parents and teachers
Before reading
Talk to the children about the eight planets in our Solar System. That is, eight planets that go round (orbit) the Sun. The Earth where we live is one of those planets. Planets which are nearer to the Sun get more of the Sun's heat. Planets which are further away from the Sun get less heat. Explain that some planets are much bigger than Earth and some are smaller.

After reading
• Make planets using play dough. Use a ball of grey dough for Mercury, orange and brown for Venus, blue and green for Earth, red for Mars, and yellow dough for Jupiter. Use light orange dough for Saturn, scoring the dough to suggest Saturn's rings. Use light blue dough for Uranus, and dark blue for Neptune. Lay out the planets in their order from the Sun: Mercury, Venus, Earth, Mars, Jupiter, Saturn, Uranus, and Neptune. Look at page 22 together to compare the sizes of different planets.
• Go on a space journey. Talk children through a dance drama based on a trip into space to see each of the planets. Set off from Earth in a spaceship and first visit the planets of Mercury and Venus which get a lot of heat from the Sun. Then turn away from the Sun and head back past Earth to view the planets of Mars, Jupiter, Saturn, Uranus, and Neptune.

24